Otsego Lake

Past and Present

THE PHOTOGRAPHS OF
RICHARD S. DUNCAN

Otsego Lake

Past and Present

THE PHOTOGRAPHS OF
RICHARD S. DUNCAN

and
Historical Images from the Collections of the
Fenimore Art Museum, Cooperstown, N.Y.

Foreword by Jane Forbes Clark
Introduction by Henry S. F. Cooper, Jr.
Edited by Paul S. D'Ambrosio

The Farmers' Museum, Inc.
Cooperstown, New York

First published in 2005 by The Farmers' Museum, Inc., Lake Road
P.O. Box 30, Cooperstown, NY 13326, http://www.farmersmuseum.org

Published in conjunction with the exhibition *Mysteries of the Lake: Otsego Lake Past and Present*, on view at The Farmers' Museum, Cooperstown, N.Y., May 18, 2004 – October 31, 2005

This book was made possible by generous contributions from Jane Forbes Clark.

Edited by Paul S. D'Ambrosio
Designed by Nadeau Design Associates, Utica, N.Y.
Printed by Brodock Press, Utica, N.Y.

FRONT COVER: Kingfisher Tower in autumn.
HALF-TITLE PAGE: Early morning fisherman.
TITLE PAGE: Looking south from Three Mile Point to Cooperstown on a clear autumn day.
CONTENTS PAGE: Sunrise over Otsego Lake, from the hills over the western shore.
OPPOSITE PAGE: Looking northeast toward Springfield from the grounds of the former Mohican Manor.
BACK COVER: Mallards in shallow water near Lakefront Park.

ISBN: 0-917334-30-2

FOREWORD

Jane Forbes Clark

Edward Clark (1811–1882), a distinguished lawyer who helped his famous client Isaac Singer protect his invention of the sewing machine and became co-founder of the Singer Sewing Machine Company, purchased large parcels of land surrounding Otsego Lake to restore and preserve the densely wooded hills.

Otsego Lake has been one of Cooperstown's most intriguing pleasures for hundreds of years. As time has rolled by on its shores, and as the seasons have changed its characteristics, the romanticism has only become deeper and more wonderful.

As Richard Duncan, Paul D'Ambrosio, and I began discussing the possibilities of publishing this book, I read a quote of my great-great-grandfather, Edward Clark, from June of 1873. The articulateness of it made me realize that this book would be a tribute to his vision for the village of Cooperstown and Lake Otsego; a vision that has carried the strong spirit of conservation and preservation of the lake and environs forward for 132 years.

> Cooperstown has a literary and romantic history, that can never be passed by or forgotten.…in my judgement it is one of the most agreeable and valuable possessions which any community can enjoy. It is our manifest interest, as it should be our greatest pleasure, to treasure up and preserve the characteristic legends of Lake Otsego and thus gradually merge fiction into fact.…I do not believe there is a fairer or more attractive spot anywhere in which to live than the classic and romantic shores of Lake Otsego.

It is a testament to Richard Duncan's artistic talent that his photographs so eloquently capture these "classic and romantic shores." With these words I leave you to enjoy this tribute to the unerring sense of conservation and preservation that defines the village and Lake Otsego.

Right: Panoramic view of Otsego Lake from the hillside above Point Judith and Kingfisher Tower, ca. 1890.

Opposite: The sun rises over the eastern hills to reveal a mist-shrouded Otsego Lake.

INTRODUCTION

Henry S. F. Cooper, Jr.

From the stone steps at Council Rock Park in Cooperstown, Otsego Lake is framed by high, largely forested hills, with one of the highest, Mount Wellington, known from its shape as "The Sleeping Lion," providing a focus at the far end. This is a classic New York State view, familiar far beyond the area. When the wind drops and the water is still, the lake is a perfect mirror of the surrounding hills; it is, in fact, also known as "The Glimmerglass," the name James Fenimore Cooper gave it in one of the Leatherstocking Tales, *The Deerslayer* (1841). For 150 years and more, most Americans, and many Europeans, got their first impressions of the American frontier from these novels. The lake – together with its surrounding hills – has been put on the National Register of Historic Places as the Glimmerglass Historic District.

James Fenimore Cooper, 1822,
by John Wesley Jarvis (ca. 1780–1840).
Oil on canvas.
Fenimore Art Museum, Cooperstown, N.Y.

Thus Otsego Lake has become a central image of the American wilderness. It may even have helped create that image, for *The Pioneers* (1823), another of the Leatherstocking Tales set around the lake, is the first example in an American novel of a view of nature as something beautiful to be preserved – as opposed to a threatening obstacle to be overcome by hard work or courage. Cooper, who grew up on its shores, derived his own feelings about nature right here, and projected them across the country and around the world in his epic novels. Hence Otsego Lake, or The Glimmerglass, together with its surrounding hills and valleys, is an American icon of Nature. It is, incidentally, an inspiration for American attitudes about conservation and environmental protection. Arguably, it is the Walden Pond of New York State.

Long before Cooper, and long afterwards, the lake has attracted people who were devoted to it. The Iroquois used it (and particularly Council Rock, a boulder at its southern end) as a meeting place; as the largest body of water in over ten thousand square miles and the source of the Susquehanna River, it was an obvious rendezvous. Traces of Iroquois settlements can still be found along its shore. James Fenimore Cooper's father, William, who founded Cooperstown in 1786, was attracted by the beauty of the lake, whose fish – in particular herring that had come upstream from the Chesapeake Bay – tided over the settlers for their first few winters. And Cooper's eldest daughter, Susan Fenimore, one of the best-known woman writers of her day, wrote lovingly of the lake, particularly in *Rural Hours* (1850), a chronicle of a year on its shores. Henry David Thoreau had a copy in his library when he was writing "Walden."

Opposite: Trees and rocks dominate the eastern shore, which is so steep in places that Cooper once noted, "a large ship might float with her yards in the forest."

Top: Natty Bumppo and Hurry Harry pass Council Rock. Felix O. C. Darley, from the 1952 edition of James Fenimore Cooper's *The Deerslayer*.

Bottom: Rowing Past Council Rock, ca. 1865.

The lake's modern era perhaps began in 1856, five years after Cooper's death, with the arrival in Cooperstown of Edward Clark, the co-founder (along with Isaac Singer) of the Singer Sewing Machine Company. That year he bought the site known as "Apple Hill" for his large Victorian stone house, "Fernleigh," just down the Susquehanna from its source in the lake. Clark began acquiring land on the lake's eastern shore, which had been largely deforested over the previous fifty years, with the conscious idea of returning it to its wilderness state – to the conditions, in fact, described in *The Deerslayer*. It is one of the earliest examples of conservation in this country. It is also landscaping and preservation on the largest scale; while American architects such as Frederick Law Olmsted were building landscaped parks comprising a square mile or so, Clark was dealing with an entire countryside, including a lake nine miles long. That he was thinking of it as an artistic unit is attested by the placement of Kingfisher Tower, which he built in 1876 two miles up the lake from Cooperstown. It provides a focus or accent for the view from the village, something he did deliberately. Edward Clark and his descendants – whose philanthropies include the Fenimore Art Museum, The Farmers' Museum, the National Baseball Hall of Fame and Museum, Bassett Healthcare, and much else – for a century and a half have conserved the lake as both a work of art and of nature.

Countless others have come to Otsego Lake, as visitors, as summer residents, and as permanent residents. As early as the 1840s, there were hundreds of literary trippers and others drawn to the lake not only by *The Leatherstocking Tales* but also by its beauty. As well as the Clarks, other families bought land around the lake, some in large chunks but many more in smaller lots; it is largely due to their devotion and care that the lake has been conserved much as it was a hundred, even two hundred, years ago. Through the centuries and the decades, and through the changing architectural styles from the Victorian to the present, *The Leatherstocking Tales* has been something of a common thread, providing names for houses, camps, boats, and even businesses, such as Mohican Lodge, Natty Bumppo, Glimmerglass Opera, and Leatherstocking Drilling Company.

For decades, conserving the lake has been a community activity of hundreds of people who live, or have lived, around its shores. The Biological Field Station of the State University of New York has researched the lake and its ecology since the mid-1960s; few lakes have been studied as intensively for as long. Several environmental groups have sprung up, such as the Otsego County Conservation Association, Otsego 2000, The Otsego Land Trust, The

Delaware-Otsego Audubon Society, the Advocates for Springfield, and others. They protect the lake against threats from within, such as pollution and unplanned development; and also from without, such as major transmission lines, windmills, and floods of motorboats. Their members seem to feel that it would be ironic if this icon of nature – and of environmental protection – should be irretrievably damaged. Even the hundreds of thousands of people who visit the National Baseball Hall of Fame and Museum, the other Cooperstown museums, and the Glimmerglass Opera, have shown their concern.

This book is about how generations of Americans have cherished and protected this Lake and its surroundings. It should give you a sense of the spirit of this place.

View from Apple Hill, 1829
Samuel F. B. Morse (1791–1872).
Oil on canvas.
Collection of Jane Forbes Clark.
In 1856 Edward Clark purchased this site and built "Fernleigh," a stone house overlooking the Susquehanna River and Otsego Lake.

Paul S. D'Ambrosio, editor

Ancient Beginnings

The placid beauty of Otsego Lake was millions of years in the making. Several important geological events formed Otsego Lake and its landscape. Between 350 and 400 million years ago, this region was the bottom of the Catskill Sea. Its waters deposited the fossil-rich sandstones and shales that make up the lower hill slopes around the lake. The great Catskill Delta, forming at the edge of the Catskill Sea, deposited the reddish sandstones at the tops of the hills.

Starting around two million years ago, massive Ice Age glaciers reshaped these hills and valleys. The ice began to advance toward present-day New York State about 23,000 years ago. Near the end of the Ice Age, valley glaciers carved long, narrow canyons as they moved southward. Like the distinctive Finger Lakes in central and western New York, Otsego Lake fills one of these Ice Age valleys. Approximately 14,000 years ago, the retreating and melting glaciers left the surface of Otsego Lake close to fifty feet higher than it is today. Modern geologists call this body of water "Glacial Lake Cooperstown." During this time, much of the lowlands around Blackbird Bay and the village of Cooperstown were submerged.

Today, Otsego Lake is a narrow body of water nine miles long, a mile and a half wide, and 168 feet deep, which makes it one of the deepest lakes in New York State. Many streams empty into the lake but underground springs are its main water source. Otsego Lake forms the headwaters of the Susquehanna River, which flows more than 400 miles to the Chesapeake Bay in Maryland.

People have lived on the shores of Otsego Lake for thousands of years. Paleolithic or "Stone Age" people left stone tools and points on the lakeshore nearly 7,000 years ago. American Indian cultures emerged here about 3,000 years ago. By 1500, the Iroquois had constructed large fortified villages across New York State. They also constructed bark houses as seasonal hunting and fishing camps on the shores of lakes such as Otsego.

The Mohawk Bark House at Fenimore Art Museum, a recreation of an Iroquois seasonal fishing camp from 1750.

Opposite: The sun and clouds form a dramatic sky over Otsego Lake in winter.

Vision in the Wilderness

I n the fall of 1785, New Jersey land speculator William Cooper traveled to Otsego Lake to investigate the potential for development in the area. Cooper later described the wilderness of Otsego Lake in *A Guide in the Wilderness*, written before 1807:

> *There existed not an inhabitant, nor any trace of a road; I was alone three hundred miles from home, without bread, meat, or food of any kind; fire and fishing were my only means of sustenance. I caught trout in the brook, and roasted them on the ashes. My horse fed on the grass that grew by the edge of the waters. I laid me down to sleep in my watch-coat, nothing but the melancholy Wilderness around me. In this way, I explored the country, formed my plans of future settlement, and meditated upon the spot where a place of trade or village should afterwards be established.*

Although the area looked wild, settlers had lived in the region since the 1740s. Several hamlets were built at the north end of the lake in the present-day town of Springfield during the 1760s. Itinerant clergyman John Christopher Hartwick, who hoped to establish a utopian community in the area, briefly occupied a clearing at the south end of the lake in 1766. In 1768, Colonel George Croghan settled at the foot of the lake hoping to establish a grand estate on the 250,000 acres he had acquired. In 1770, he fled to escape his debts. After the Revolutionary War, a few settlers arrived, most of whom were hunters and squatters who never held a title to the land they occupied.

In 1786, Cooper acquired much of Croghan's land and began laying out the streets of Cooperstown. He sold village lots and farm properties outright to the new settlers, rather than leasing properties in the tradition of landed estates. By 1790, the village was beginning to take shape: there were thirty-five residents, seven houses, three barns, one store, and one tavern. One of those villagers who grew up exploring every point, bay, and creek of the lake he loved was William's son, James Cooper, who later adopted the middle name Fenimore.

William Cooper, 1794,
by Gilbert Stuart (1755-1828).
Oil on canvas.
Fenimore Art Museum, Cooperstown, N.Y.

Opposite: The densely wooded hills of the eastern shore ablaze with color at the height of autumn.

A Region of Romance

Nature and history shaped Otsego Lake, but it was a pen and an extraordinary imagination that brought it to life for those who had not visited its shores nor heard of the little village of Cooperstown. Through his novels, James Fenimore Cooper made Otsego Lake known the world over as a setting for romance and adventure.

Cooper wrote five immensely popular *Leatherstocking Tales* between 1823 and 1841. Two of the *Tales* take place on and around Otsego Lake, called "The Glimmerglass" by Cooper for its mirror-like surface. The lake and its surrounding landscape are central to the novels, and are as important as the characters in driving the action.

The Pioneers (1823) introduces the frontier hero Natty Bumppo or "Leatherstocking," one of literature's most enduring characters. *The Pioneers* also describes the frontier village "Templeton," modeled on Cooperstown, just as it is beginning to prosper.

The last of *The Leatherstocking Tales*, *The Deerslayer* (1841), introduces a young Natty Bumppo, then called "Deerslayer." The story takes place long before Cooperstown was settled, and Deerslayer is just learning the ways of the forest. Vivid descriptions of the lake and its surrounding hills and streams fill the novel. Cooper punctuates his serene descriptions of the natural landscape with episodes of violence and horror as frontiersmen, soldiers, and Indians fight for control of the lake.

James Fenimore Cooper had predicted and encouraged tourism as early as the 1830s, but it was his widely read *Leatherstocking Tales* that enticed visitors to come to the area. The first serious investors in Otsego Lake tourism capitalized on Cooper's legacy by promoting sites made famous in the novels. New hotels, steamboats, streets, businesses, and sites on the lake were given names inspired by *The Leatherstocking Tales*.

"All this while the canoe, with the form of Hetty erect in one end of it, was dimly perceptible." Illustration by N. C. Wyeth, from *The Deerslayer* by James Fenimore Cooper, 1925 edition.

Opposite: The lake's western shore slopes gently down to the water and features a number of peninsulas, such as this one at Brookwood, two miles north of Cooperstown.

Preserving a Legacy

Photographer Arthur J. Telfer
at Kingfisher Tower, ca. 1910.

The Otsego Lake landscape was one of the earliest in America to be actively protected. William Cooper commented on the loss of forestland as his settlement grew, and his son James Fenimore Cooper described wasteful hunting and fishing practices in his novels. James Fenimore Cooper's daughter, Susan Fenimore Cooper, published one of the earliest examples of American nature writing, *Rural Hours* (1850), four years before Henry David Thoreau's *Walden*. She too decried the thoughtless cutting of trees and documented the great changes in the natural landscape that had occurred since her grandfather had founded Cooperstown.

Efforts made by generations of the Clark family, beginning with Edward Clark in the 1870s, have helped preserve the natural environment of Otsego Lake. Clark had amassed a considerable fortune as a partner in the Singer Sewing Machine Company and began to acquire property around the lake where his wife, Caroline Jordan Clark, had been raised. Inspired by the natural beauty of Otsego Lake and the legacy of Cooper, Clark built a chalet-style camp on Point Judith in 1875 and the castle-like Kingfisher Tower in 1876, simply for pleasure.

> *[Kingfisher Tower] adds solemnity to the landscape, seeming to stand guard over the vicinity, while it gives a character of antiquity to the lake. The effect of the structure is that of a picture from medieval times, and its value to the lake is very great. Mr. Clark has been led to erect it simply by a desire to beautify the lake.*
>
> The Freeman's Journal, 7 September 1876

The Clark family has owned much of the eastern shore of the lake since the early 1900s and has acquired several important parcels on the western shore since the 1950s. Cleared areas on the eastern shore were allowed to reforest, eventually taking on the appearance of the environment described in *The Deerslayer*.

Today there are numerous organizations and individuals working to protect Otsego Lake. In 1999, their combined efforts led to the addition of the Glimmerglass Historic District to the National Register of Historic Places. It is a 15,000-acre district that includes all of Otsego Lake, portions of the towns of Otsego, Middlefield and Springfield, and the entire village of Cooperstown.

Opposite: In an image that exemplifies Edward Clark's vision, Kingfisher Tower lends an aura of antiquity to a landscape carefully restored to the condition of the primeval amphitheater of Cooper's *The Deerslayer*.

Tourism and Recreation

Otsego Lake holds a special place in the memories of generations of campers, picnickers, and fishermen. One of the first known Otsego Lake boating parties was given by William Cooper in 1799. He organized canoes and flat-bottomed skiffs to carry a picnic party of twenty-five to "Two Mile Point," now called Point Judith and the present site of Kingfisher Tower.

Transportation began to improve in the 1850s, and more people came to the area. They enjoyed the same activities that we enjoy today: boating, camping, fishing, picnicking, swimming, scenic drives, and walks.

The arrival of the railroad in 1869 led to a surge in summer visitation. In response, entrepreneurs constructed larger and more fashionable hotels and improved recreation facilities. Steamships carried people the length of the lake and on pleasure trips. By the early 1870s, luxury hotels catered to every need and advertised their proximity to Otsego Lake.

At the same time, rustic camping holidays became popular. Camps on the lake ranged from primitive tent platforms and simple cabins to elaborate cottages and two-story structures built over the water. They were enjoyed by area residents and rented out to visitors. By the 1880s, several substantial camps had been built to accommodate large camping parties.

Overnight camps for children were established in the 1910s. They included Pathfinder's Lodge for girls, the Ethical Culture School for boys and girls, and Pickett's Camp for boys, which opened in 1926 in Hyde Bay. Pickett's ran a canoe trip around the lake during which the boys were "instructed in the lore of the Leatherstocking land." Lester G. Bursey ran the Cooperstown Playground Program for more than 40 years beginning in the 1920s. This day camp included Red Cross swim lessons at Three Mile Point in the morning and activities at the Cooperstown Elementary School in the afternoon.

To make the beauty of Otsego Lake accessible to a broad public, the State of New York created Glimmerglass State Park in 1963 with the purchase of 600 acres at the north end of the lake. Each year more than 100,000 people visit Glimmerglass State Park to swim, picnic, hike, ski, snowshoe, or compete in the annual Glimmerglass Triathlon.

Top: Walrath and Gazley, photographed about 1915 with the day's catch. Stokes Gazley was the son of Armond Gazley, who ran a large boatyard in Blackbird Bay until 1909.

Bottom: Two young campers relax on their bunks at Camp Fenimore, near Fairy Spring, 1930.

Opposite: Sailing vessels moored at the Otsego Sailing Club on a calm summer day, with Cooperstown in the distance.

Steamboats on Otsego Lake

Top: Launched in July 1871, the *Natty Bumppo* was the largest ship on Otsego Lake. She was destroyed by fire in 1872, and quickly replaced by a new steamboat with the same name. The second *Natty Bumppo*, which operated from about 1872 until 1898, is pictured here at the lakefront in Cooperstown.

Bottom: Otsego Lake Steamboat Company Stage on the shore of the lake in Springfield, N.Y., ca. 1890.

The first steamboat on Otsego Lake was launched in 1858. The *Pioneer* was an experimental pleasure boat and made only a few voyages, yet its presence on the lake prompted the local newspaper to announce, *Who says we are not living in a progressive age?* In 1869, D. B. Boden launched the *Mary Boden*, a refurbished Civil War gun boat thirty-eight feet long and used principally as a pleasure boat.

By 1870, railroads had reached the villages of Cooperstown and Richfield Springs, a six-mile stagecoach ride northwest of Springfield Center which is at the northern end of the lake. However, if a visitor wanted to get from Richfield Springs to Cooperstown, they faced an additional nine-mile stagecoach ride along the muddy, bumpy lake road. Businessmen and investors realized that a nine-mile boat ride down Otsego Lake would be much more comfortable and pleasurable for visitors. In response, the *Natty Bumppo*, a commercial passenger ship, was launched in July of 1871. She was ninety feet long and could carry 300 people under two covered decks. In the height of the summer, the *Natty Bumppo* made three trips a day up and down Otsego Lake to meet coaches from Richfield Springs, Springfield Center, and Cooperstown. She made stops at Three and Five Mile Points. The *Natty Bumppo* was destroyed by fire in 1872 but was quickly replaced by the *Natty Bumppo II*, the largest ship on Otsego Lake.

By the late 1800s, "steamers" ran almost around the clock, six days per week, in the summer months. Special excursions and moonlit rides were offered, and summer residents could purchase books of discounted tickets. Additionally, public steamboat landings such as Otsego Lake Park (now Lakefront Park) in Cooperstown, and Island Cottage in Springfield Center were popular recreation areas where visitors could rent boats, have a picnic, or go to a restaurant. The Otsego Lake Transit Company, established in 1905, was the last steamboat company to be formed on the lake. It ran its own line of stagecoaches between connections and along Otsego Lake.

By the 1930s, automobiles, improved roads, and personal powerboats forced steamboat companies out of business. Since then, recreational boats have carried seasonal sightseers the length of Otsego Lake.

Opposite: Launching the steamboat *Mohican*, 1905.

A Row Around the Lake

In 1936 James Fenimore Cooper, grandson of the novelist, published a short paper for the Otsego County Historical Society that described a mid-nineteenth-century tradition for viewing Otsego Lake. He explains how one would rent a livery boat at the lakefront in Cooperstown and spend all day rowing the twenty-three miles around the lake, first moving northward along the western shore and then southward along the wooded eastern banks. This book takes the reader on a similar journey – less tiring, perhaps, but equally fascinating – to each of the principal sites on the lake. Each stop on this pictorial row around the lake reveals the beauty, history, and mystery of Otsego Lake, as well as the extraordinary cast of characters that makes it unique.

Above: Two fashionably dressed Victorian ladies
enjoy the lake in a livery boat, ca. 1890.

Opposite: View of Otsego Lake looking north from West Hill.
This elevated perspective from a hill overlooking Cooperstown shows the irregular
outline of the western shore and Mount Wellington in the distance.

1 Cooperstown

2 Blackbird Bay

3 Three Mile Point

7 Hyde Bay

8 Pegg's Point

9 Gravelly Point

4 Five Mile Point

5 Springfield

6 Mount Wellington

10 Point Judith

11 Fairy Spring

12 Council Rock

SEGO LAKE

Sunken Island

MIDDLEFIELD

COOPERSTOWN

"What romantic beauties here;
how does nature flourish
and outstrip every conception.
A morning equal to any in May;
a most superb range
of mountains approaching
by a gradual descent to the water;
a beautiful large lake below,
as transparent as crystal
and as smooth as a sea of glass."

Griffith Evans
2 November 1784

Crowds gathered at the lakefront boat livery
pose for a group photograph, ca. 1870.

COOPERSTOWN

The lakefront has been an important feature of Cooperstown from its founding in 1786 until the present day. Although the village was named after its founder, William Cooper, it was also called "Foot of the Lake" for many years. The lakefront has evolved from a site of industry and transportation to one of recreation and access to the lake.

In 1786, a single family lived at the foot of Otsego Lake. Four years later, there were eight families in the area. When Cooperstown was named the county seat in 1791, more people were drawn to the village. By 1796, there were fifty-five houses, three inns, four stores and more than fifteen different tradesmen in Cooperstown.

The easy availability of water was important to the early residents of Cooperstown. Many tradesmen who needed access to fresh water established businesses near the lakeshore. From the 1780s through the early 1800s, a tannery, brewery, bathhouse, boat dock, boat repair shop, and paint shop were all established near the lakefront. In 1800, William Cooper and others formed the Company of Water Works to provide drinking water to the village. However, an efficient system was not established until 1880 when the Cooperstown Aqueduct Association built a pump house.

Otsego Lake is still the source of drinking water for Cooperstown residents and visitors. The current Otsego Lake Watershed Council uses State of New York guidelines to ensure the quality of the drinking water drawn from Otsego Lake. During the summer, 900,000 gallons of water are used everyday.

Transportation was an important lakefront industry. In the 1850s, Captain P. P. Cooper established a popular boat dock at the foot of present-day Pioneer Street. He offered lake parties on his boat, *The Swan*, and provided a small boat rental service. Steamboats also met passengers at a number of boat docks at the village lakefront.

By about 1900, access to Otsego Lake was nearly limited to those owning or renting lakeshore property. To provide better public access, Otsego Lake Park was created in 1902 on the former Captain P. P. Cooper property. The present Lakefront Park opened on August 10, 1938. The park features terraced lawns, gravel paths, a bandstand and, since 1940, a copy of a famous bronze sculpture by John Quincy Adams Ward entitled *Indian Hunter*. Today, it is Cooperstown's most popular site for picnics, boat-watching, and public concerts.

Top: The village of Cooperstown from a hillside above the eastern shore of Otsego Lake, ca. 1870.

Bottom: Otsego Lake Park on Regatta Day, ca. 1905.

Opposite: The dock at the Otesaga Hotel with the Lake Front Marina in the distance.

Above: A spectacular summer evening occurs every Fourth of July when thousands of spectators enjoy fireworks from a variety of vantage points, including their boats.

Opposite: The Lake Front Marina, one of two boatyards on Otsego Lake, seen on a placid summer day.

Above: A manicured lawn, Otsego Lake, and Star Field on the east side
provide the setting as photographer Charles Zabriskie poses his daughter Anita with an
Oriental parasol on the grounds of his lakefront estate, "Glimmerview," ca. 1900.

Opposite: A number of private residences on the lakefront in
Cooperstown still feature lush, colorful grounds and striking views of the lake.

The village of Cooperstown nestled at the southern end of Otsego Lake.

Above: Otsego Lake, called the *Glimmerglass* by James Fenimore Cooper, is famed for its reflections. Here the Otesaga Resort Hotel, built in 1909, casts its image onto the waters on a quiet autumn day.

Opposite: John Quincy Adams Ward's *Indian Hunter* looks out over Lakefront Park on a misty morning in late summer.

Above: Mallards are a common sight on the lake, in the parks,
and even on the streets of the village.

Opposite: A lone sailboat at the Lake Front Marina,
with the sun rising over Mount Vision.

Above: The Lighthouse at the Lake Front Marina is
one of the most prominent features of the lakefront at Cooperstown.

Opposite: The light of a clear, crisp winter morning catches
the frosty docks at the Marina and the hillside along the eastern shore.

BLACKBIRD BAY

*"The placid water swept round
in a graceful curve,
the rushes bent gently towards
its surface, and the trees
overhung it as usual...
all lay in the soothing and
sublime solitude of a wilderness.
The scene was such
as a poet or an artist would
have delighted in..."*

The Deerslayer, Chapter III

Aerial view of Blackbird Bay with the
Otesaga Hotel in the foreground, 1939.

BLACKBIRD BAY

Blackbird Bay lies less than a mile from Cooperstown on the western shore of the lake. The bay was once nearly enclosed by a small peninsula. In the late nineteenth century, the Gazley boatyard and docks dominated the bay. The entire area was dramatically altered around 1909 with the construction of the Otesaga Hotel, the Leatherstocking Golf Course and the Cooperstown Country Club.

In *The Pioneers*, Cooper set the annual bass fishing expedition in Blackbird Bay. The narrator and Natty Bumppo are opposed to net fishing, calling it both destructive and wasteful. The Sheriff promotes net fishing, and the Judge suggests smaller nets as a compromise.

Like the residents of the fictitious Templeton in *The Pioneers*, the residents of 19th-century Cooperstown argued about various fishing methods. Net fishing was hotly debated in regular articles and letters in *The Freeman's Journal*. Many feared the depletion of the carefully stocked fish population while others saw the fish as a resource to be taken by any method available. Around 1900, net fishing was outlawed and remains illegal today.

Right: Boating in the shallows of Blackbird Bay, ca. 1900.

Opposite: Although its outline has greatly changed in the past 100 years, Blackbird Bay still features undulating curves and marshy areas. This view shows the golf course sweeping along the bay from the Otesaga Hotel to the Cooperstown Country Club.

Above: Autumn leaves swaying gently in the undercurrent in the shallow water.

Opposite: A lone tree overlooking Blackbird Bay.

Top: Looking across Blackbird Bay from the Otesaga Hotel to the Cooperstown Country Club, ca. 1920.

Bottom: Construction of the Leatherstocking Golf Course, 1909. This par 72 course was designed in 1909 by Devereux Emmet. Adjacent to the Otesaga Hotel, the course hugs the shore of Blackbird Bay and then climbs hilly terrain just northwest of the bay. It is now considered one of the premier golf courses in the United States.

Opposite: Sand trap at the 18th hole on the Leatherstocking Golf Course.

Above: Gazley Boatyard in Blackbird Bay, before 1909. Located at the end of Nelson Avenue, this yard was a busy center of activity until just after the turn of the 20th century. The boatyard closed with the construction of the Otesaga Hotel and the Leatherstocking Golf Course.

Opposite: The dock at the Cooperstown Country Club on a foggy morning.

Above: Elevated view of the Leatherstocking Golf Course at dawn,
with the Lake Front Marina in the distance.

Opposite: Bridge to the island tee at the 18th hole, seen in
early winter as the ice begins to form in the bay.

Above: A pair of trees on the golf course appear to be holding hands.

Opposite: Looking north from Blackbird Bay to Mount Wellington.

Above and opposite: The pastures above the Lippitt Farmstead
at The Farmers' Museum offer the opportunity to step into the past while enjoying
stunning views of Blackbird Bay, Otsego Lake, and the village of Cooperstown.

THREE MILE POINT

"The whole projection into the lake

contained about two acres

of land.... It was principally covered

with oaks, which, as is usual

in the American forests, grew to

a great height without

throwing out a branch, and then

arched in a dense and

rich foliage.... The surface of the

land was tolerably even,

but it had a small rise near its

center, which divided it

into a northern and southern half....

A brook also came brawling

down the sides of the adjacent hills,

and found its way into the lake

on the southern side of the point."

The Deerslayer, Chapter XVI

Cookout at
Three Mile Point, ca.1870.

33

THREE MILE POINT

*The family all spent the day at Three Mile Point on Thursday…
and enjoyed themselves abundantly. Friday, the Musical Association
gave a Pic Nic at the same place…*   John Holmes Prentiss to daughter
Charlotte Prentiss, July 20, 1857

Three Mile Point provides the most striking panoramic views of the entire lake from Mount Wellington to the village of Cooperstown. Its natural beauty and low stretch of open land extending into the lake made the point ideal for large picnics. In the nineteenth century, Cooperstown residents enjoyed a tradition of holding lake parties using a large rowing skiff to ferry picnickers from the village to the point.

The Cooper family owned the property from the early 1800s and called it "Myrtle Grove." The point became the subject of controversy when James Fenimore Cooper returned from Europe in the 1830s. He found that the point had been used by the public and had, in his opinion, suffered extensive damage. He ran a chain across the point and published a notice in the newspaper forbidding access.

Cooper provoked such public anger that some threatened to remove his books from the local library. Newspapers across New York State denounced Cooper's actions, although he acted within his legal rights. Cooper sued these newspapers for libel, acted as his own lawyer, and won each case.

The point remained the property of the Cooper family for many years. In 1871, William Storrs Cooper leased the property to the Cooperstown Village Improvement Society. The Village of Cooperstown purchased the property in 1899 and it has been a popular park ever since.

Above: "Joe Tom," ca. 1870. John Thomas Husbands emigrated from Barbados to Cooperstown. He was a renowned chef and catered most of the lake parties held at Three Mile Point in the mid-19th century.

Left: The picnic pavilion on the north side of the point, with Mount Wellington in the distance.

Opposite: The beach and dock at Three Mile Point, owned by the Village of Cooperstown, is a popular summer recreation area. Here, a few early swimmers take advantage of the relative quiet of a summer morning.

Top: This photograph from the 1860s shows an actual
lake party on Three Mile Point, similar to the scene painted
at right in the 1850s.

Above: The Three Mile Point House, situated above the point
on an adjoining hillside, was famous for its fish and game dinners.
This photograph was probably taken in the 1860s.

Opposite: Lake Party at Three Mile Point, ca. 1855, by
Louis Remy Mignot (1831–1870) and Julius Gollmann (d. 1898).
Oil on canvas.
Fenimore Art Museum, Cooperstown, N.Y.
Many prominent Cooperstown and Cherry Valley residents appear
in the painting, which depicts the popular pastime of lake parties.

The topography of Three Mile Point is much the same today as it was in the mid-19th century.
The vintage tour boat *Uncas* and the boathouse at right are owned by the Busch family.

Above: Patriotic bunting adds a festive touch to the Bath House.

Opposite: Young beachcombers fill the moat
around their sandcastle on a bright summer afternoon.

Right and below: Victorian boaters enjoy an excursion to Three Mile Point in the 1860s.

Opposite: The shoreline south of Three Mile Point in full autumn glory.

Above and opposite: Three Mile Point in winter, seen from the north.

FIVE MILE POINT

"The Five-Mile Point House,
situated on Otsego Lake,
five miles from Cooperstown,
burned to the ground
Sunday night. Messrs. Wedderspoon
& Whipple announce that
they will, for the present, continue
to serve dinners under
a large tent to be erected upon
the lawn of the Point,
across the road from the site
of the hotel."

Freeman's Journal
30 July 1908

Bathing at Five Mile Point, ca. 1900.

FIVE MILE POINT

Five Mile Point provides a sweeping view of Mount Wellington and Hyde Bay from the western shore of the lake. Generations of residents and visitors enjoyed gathering at the point.

In 1851, John D. Tunnicliff converted a farmhouse on the point into an inn and tavern, which he ran for nearly forty years. By the late 1870s, several families had established camps on or near Five Mile Point and Tunnicliff's Inn had become famous for its fish and game dinners.

In 1902, M. H. Wedderspoon and J. D. Whipple purchased and improved the inn, by then called the Five Mile Point House. Only six years later, fire destroyed the inn in the middle of the summer season. The Cooperstown Fire Department arrived by boat, but could not save the building.

Wedderspoon and Whipple set up a large pavilion and resumed the dinners within a week, but soon agreed to sell the property for a private residence. A group of local citizens, concerned that the point would lose its function as a public gathering place, raised $15,000 in less than two hours to meet the purchase price. The group formed the Five-Mile Point Hotel Company and built a new inn, which opened on July 1, 1909. The second Five Mile Point House was never as popular as the first, and was sold to a private owner in 1918. The point remains private property today.

A famous, if fictional, visitor to Five Mile Point was teen sleuth Nancy Drew. In the 1972 mystery, *The Secret of Mirror Bay*, Nancy finds a cryptic poem that leads her to Five Mile Point. From there, she is led to Hyde Bay, where she discovers a Russian pony carriage that had been hidden in the lake years earlier. At the end of the novel, the rightful owner of the carriage presents it to the "Fenimore Museum," where it is accepted by "Mr. Clark."

Right: The Five Mile Point House seen from the north, ca. 1870.

Opposite: Five Mile Point from the south on an autumn morning.

The Five-Mile Point House, situated on Otsego Lake, five miles from Cooperstown, burned to the ground Sunday night. The larger portion of the furniture on the first floor was saved. The loss is estimated at $12,000, with insurance of $4,000. Messrs. Wedderspoon & Whipple announce that they will, for the present, continue to serve dinners under a large tent to be erected upon the lawn of the Point, across the road from the site of the hotel. A temporary kitchen is being constructed and they hope to be ready for business the latter part of this week.

Freeman's Journal
30 July 1908

Top: Five Mile Point House, before the 1908 fire.

Bottom: Five Mile Point House as rebuilt after the fire.

Opposite: The point remains private property today, and features boating and recreation areas for owners of Glimmerglass Condominiums on the hillside above.

Above: Camp Mohican, 1897. One of the oldest surviving
private camps on Otsego Lake, Camp Mohican sits on a small peninsula
about one-half mile south of Five Mile Point.

Opposite: Camp Mohican today.

Above: This stone arch marks the passage of an old road
that brought visitors to the Five Mile Point House.

Opposite: One of the most distinctive features of Five Mile Point,
visible from a distance in any direction, is the large willow tree whose branches
extend beyond the edge of the peninsula and over the water.

Above: The Bunn family at Five Mile Point, 1912.

Opposite: The willow tree in the full bloom of summer.

Above: A lone chair at the end of the point
overlooks Mount Wellington and Hyde Bay to the northeast.

Opposite: A variety of camps large and
small crowd the shoreline north of Five Mile Point.

SPRINGFIELD

★

"Looking back one hundred and fifteen years, to the year 1762, we find this pleasant and prosperous town, with its many comfortable habitations, its schoolhouses and its sanctuaries, its sweet hills and cultured vales, one unbroken wilderness, a wild and romantic country indeed."

History of Otsego County, 1878

Dakin family and friends at Springfield Center, 1888.

61

SPRINGFIELD

Top: Steamer *Natty Bumppo*
at Springfield Landing, ca. 1870.

Bottom: Springfield Landing Dock, ca. 1930.
Springfield Historical Society

The Town of Springfield includes nearly all of Hyde Bay on the eastern shore of the lake and extends almost to Six Mile Point on the western shore. Mount Wellington, Hyde Hall and Glimmerglass State Park are all located in Springfield. The town consists of the villages of Springfield Center, Springfield, and East Springfield. Today the town has 1,350 year-round residents.

Springfield is one of the earliest settlements on Otsego Lake. One of the first recorded trips there was made in 1737 by Cadwallader Colden, then surveyor-general for the Province of New York. In 1762, five families settled in the area. By 1767, they had been joined by five more families.

In the 1800s, Springfield Center was an important stop for stagecoaches traveling between Cooperstown and the Cherry Valley Turnpike to the north. From the 1870s through the early 1900s, Tally-Ho stage coaches carried passengers from the railroad station in Richfield Springs to Otsego Lake where passengers could board Otsego Lake steamboats at the landing called "Island Cottage."

The Public Landing in Springfield opened at the base of Mount Wellington in about 1930. It was used for a short time by Otsego Lake steamboats and is now a boat launch and recreation area for the residents of Springfield.

There are many beautiful summer estates in Springfield including Swanswick built in the 1790s, Cary Mede built in 1889, and Pinehurst built about 1890. In 1894, the 12-hole Otsego Golf Club opened on lakefront property owned by Leslie Pell-Clarke (Swanswick) and Henry L. Wardwell (Pinehurst), two of the principal founders of the club. The Otsego Golf Club, now a 9-hole course owned by the Head of the Lake Corporation, is one of the oldest courses in the United States.

The Glimmerglass Opera Company, which each year since 1975 has mounted a major summer opera festival, in 1987 found a new home at the former Cary Mede Farm property. In that year the company, whose productions had formerly been staged in the Cooperstown High School, launched its first season in the new Alice Busch Opera Theater, the first American Hall built specifically for opera since 1966. The design of the theater was inspired by local barn architecture. Glimmerglass Opera presents more than forty performances of four productions in repertory every summer.

Opposite: This elevated view of a farm in the foreground and the Alice Busch Opera Theater of the Glimmerglass Opera Company in the distance symbolizes Springfield's agricultural heritage and current cultural importance.

Above: A remnant of Springfield's past perched high above the lake
at the former Thayer farm, now the property of the Biological Field Station
of the State University of New York College at Oneonta.

Opposite: Taken just before the spring thaw, this photograph shows
the still-frozen waters of Otsego Lake at its northern end.

Above: A lone heron sits quietly by the shoreline.

Opposite: The setting sun illuminates the western side
of Mount Wellington, creating a striking visual effect.

Above: A flock of Canada geese takes to the air on a crisp autumn day.

Opposite: Twin birches waiting for spring.

Above: An ornamental fish weathervane graces the roof of a camp near Springfield.

Opposite: A low peninsula juts out into shallow water
on the grounds of the former Mohican Manor.

Above: The garden at Swanswick, one of the oldest private estates in Springfield.

Opposite: The boathouse at Cary Mede, a private estate.

Above: Private dock near the Otsego Golf Club on a quiet autumn day.

Opposite: With an elegance that complements the landscape, a vintage canoe rests on the edge of a shallow creek near the Otsego Golf Club.

Mount Wellington seen
from Otsego Lake Park, 1905.

MOUNT WELLINGTON

*"...it was bounded by
an isolated mountain,
lower land falling off
east and west,
gracefully relieving
the sweep
of the outline..."*

The Deerslayer, Chapter II

MOUNT WELLINGTON

Mount Wellington dominates views of the northern shores of Otsego Lake. Thousands of years ago, glaciers swept down the sides of the mountain, carving out the well-defined profile as they retreated. The hill was named by George Hyde Clarke for his classmate, the Duke of Wellington, but its familiar profile from the village of Cooperstown gives it the popular name "Sleeping Lion." Today, hikers may explore the 520-foot-high Mount Wellington, which is within Glimmerglass State Park.

Above: Looking north toward Mount Wellington, 1935.

Opposite: Sailboat at rest on the placid waters of Otsego Lake, with Mount Wellington looming in the distance. Kingfisher Tower is visible at the right.

Above: Clarke Point, the southernmost edge of Mount Wellington, from the hillside pasture of the former Thayer Farm in Springfield.

Opposite: The shallow water of Lakefront Park in Cooperstown recedes gracefully to a distant view of the Sleeping Lion.

Above: The rising sun reveals the contours
of Mount Wellington on a misty autumn morning.

Opposite: The Sleeping Lion in winter, from a vantage point that shows
the stretches of lowland to either side, the result of the
mountain's formation by receding glaciers thousands of years ago.

Left and below: Viewed from high and low, near and far, Mount Wellington retains its distinctive shape in these photographs from about 1900.

Opposite: Sleeping Lion as seen from Blackbird Bay.

Above: The lake's bounty knows no season. Here,
ice fishermen check their lines and take in an expansive winter landscape.

Opposite: A young fisherman shows off his prize catch.

HYDE BAY

"Into this bay from the east
flows Shadow Brook,
the most picturesque stream
of water in the region,
whose pellucid current reflects
clear images of foliage and
sky, and offers a favorite resort,
in its shaded nooks,
to the drifting canoes of lovers."

The Story of Cooperstown, 1917
Ralph Birdsall

Looking down Shadow Brook
to Otsego Lake, ca. 1880.

89

HYDE BAY

Top: Cottage at Hyde Bay, ca. 1910.
Some cottages were literally on the water.

Bottom: "Sous les Bois" cabin, Ethical Culture
camp, late 1920s. The Ethical Culture camp
for boys and girls opened in 1923.

Hyde Bay is located at the northeastern end of Otsego Lake. At the beginning of *The Deerslayer*, Hurry Harry and Deerslayer (Natty Bumppo) break through the forest and swamp to reach the lake at this spot. Shadow Brook, called "the most picturesque stream of water in the region," flows into Hyde Bay from the east. The stream's still waters perfectly reflect the sky and the shadows of overhanging trees.

The bay takes its name from George Hyde Clarke, an English-born American citizen, who inherited more than 50,000 acres in central New York. Clarke hired architect Philip Hooker of Albany to design a Regency-style country house overlooking the bay. Hyde Hall, built between 1819 and 1835 of local limestone, is a British-inspired country estate. The house features forty main rooms, some with eighteen-foot ceilings and quartz-dusted walls that shimmer in candle-light. Clarke family members lived at Hyde Hall until the 1960s.

Hyde Bay has been a popular picnic and recreation site for over a century. In the early 1900s, the locally formed Hyde Bay Association bought several acres of lakefront from the Clarke family and built a picnic pavilion, steamboat dock and overnight cabins.

The State of New York created Glimmerglass State Park in 1963 with the purchase of 600 acres of the George Hyde Clarke estate. When New York State acquired the property, Hyde Hall faced demolition. The Friends of Hyde Hall formed in 1964 to ensure the preservation and restoration of the Clarke mansion. Due to their efforts, Hyde Hall was saved and is open to the public today. A restoration work-in-progress, it is considered by architecture critics to be one of the greatest structures built in its time in America.

Right: Picnic Lodge, Hyde Bay Association
Picnic Grounds, 1916.

Opposite: View of Hyde Bay from the fields
at Glimmerglass State Park, looking south
towards Pegg's Point.

Above: Clarke-Choate wedding at Hyde Hall, 1907.

Opposite: The porch at Hyde Hall commands a view southward
down the entire length of Otsego Lake.

Above: An alert mallard drake finds a convenient perch in the shallow water.

Opposite: A flock of Canada geese floats in
Hyde Bay near the point where Shadow Brook flows into the lake.

Above: The docks at Hyde Bay Landing,
seen in a 1910 postcard and a photograph from the 1930s.

Opposite: Hyde Bay Landing played an important role in steam transportation
from points north and east of the lake to Cooperstown at the southern end.

Above: Ice fishermen and dogs with their homemade shanty, ca. 1910.

Opposite: Two travelers and their dog trek southward from Hyde Bay across the frozen lake.

PEGG'S POINT & GRAVELLY POINT

*"The soldiers too had taken
up their line of march;
first setting the ark adrift again,
with a reckless disregard
of its fate. All this Judith saw,
but she heeded it not.
The Glimmerglass had no longer
any charms for her;
and when she put her foot
on the strand, she immediately
proceeded on the trail
of the soldiers, without casting
a single glance behind her."*

The Deerslayer, Chapter XXXII

Cherry Valley residents
at Gravelly Point, ca. 1900.

PEGG'S POINT AND GRAVELLY POINT

Pegg's Point forms the southern entrance to Hyde Bay, and provides a northwestern view of the lake. It takes its name from Thomas Pegg, who owned the land and ran a tavern nearby on the Otsego Lake Turnpike in the mid-nineteenth century. The point was once a popular camping and picnic spot. It is now private property.

Cooper chose to begin and end the main action of *The Deerslayer* at Pegg's Point. Early in the novel, Hurry Harry and Natty Bumppo leave Pegg's Point to begin their canoe trip across the lake. Near the close of the novel Deerslayer (Bumppo), his companions, and the British troops that rescued them leave Otsego Lake from Pegg's Point:

> *As neither [Judith nor Natty] laboured hard at the paddle, the ark had already arrived, and the soldiers had disembarked...All this, Judith saw; but she heeded it not. The Glimmerglass had no longer any charms for her; and when she put her foot on the strand, she immediately proceeded on the trail of the soldiers, without casting a single glance behind her.*
>
> —*The Deerslayer*, James Fenimore Cooper

Natty Bumppo's transformation from the young novice known as Deerslayer to an experienced woodsman takes place on Gravelly Point, approximately one-half mile south of Pegg's Point. Here he gains the name Hawkeye, by which he is known in the later *Leatherstocking Tales*. In pursuit of a drifting canoe, Deerslayer approaches this exposed point. He is forced to exchange gunfire with an Indian waiting to steal the canoe. Deerslayer mortally wounds the Indian, but holds the dying man so that he may drink water from the lake. With his dying breath, the Indian gives his opponent the name "Hawkeye." In 1911, the Vitagraph Company recreated this scene at Gravelly Point for the movie version of *The Deerslayer*.

Gravelly Point is about six miles from Cooperstown on the eastern shore. In the 1870s, many rustic campgrounds were located in this area. Today, it is private property.

Top: Natty Bumppo's encounter on Gravelly Point. This photograph dates from the 1911 filming of *The Deerslayer*, shot on location on Otsego Lake.

Bottom: Gravelly Point in a 1910 postcard.

Opposite: Pegg's Point on a breezy summer day.

Top: The Peevers children
at Gravelly Point, August 1931.

Bottom: A family at
Gravelly Point, ca. 1930.

Opposite: This private camp at
Gravelly Point blends harmoniously
into the landscape.

Top: A group poses by the shoreline at Gravelly Point, ca. 1910.

Bottom: Little Gravelly Camp (Bronx) about 1910. Rustic camping in the early 20th century was much more formal than modern campers might expect.

Opposite: The steep shoreline south of Gravelly Point hints at the depth of the water nearby, which at more than 160 feet is the deepest in the lake.

Top: Girl Scouts at Gravelly Point, ca. 1920.

Bottom: The wildness of the shoreline at Gravelly Point, ca. 1900.

Opposite: Pegg's Point from across Hyde Bay to the north.

POINT JUDITH

*"It forms an objective point
in the scene presented by
the lake and surrounding hills;
it adds solemnity to the
landscape, seeming to stand
guard over the vicinity,
while it gives a character of
antiquity to the lake,
a charm by which we cannot
help being impressed
in such scenes....The effect of
the structure is that of
a picture from medieval times,
and its value to the lake
is very great."*

Edward Clark
Freeman's Journal, 7 Sept. 1876

Centennial Picnic at Point Judith, August 1899.
This photograph recorded the one hundredth
anniversary of William Cooper's first "lake party."
The well-dressed guests were descendents
of the original participants and were invited
to Point Judith by Edward Clark.

POINT JUDITH

P oint Judith is located about two miles north of Cooperstown on the eastern shore and was originally called Two Mile Point. Judge William Cooper hosted the first recorded lake party here in August 1799. The guests arrived aboard canoes and flat-bottomed skiffs. A century later, descendants of those early picnickers arrived by steamboat to commemorate the 1799 excursion.

Edward Clark renamed Two Mile Point as Point Judith, after Judith Hutter from James Fenimore Cooper's *The Deerslayer*. This is the place where Natty Bumppo finds the abandoned Ark, the houseboat once inhabited by Judith, her sister Hetty, and their father, Tom.

In 1875, Edward Clark purchased the property and commissioned New York architect Henry J. Hardenburgh to design and construct a lodge and small medieval-style tower at the end of Point Judith. Sixty feet high, with a foundation reinforced against the forces of winter ice, Kingfisher Tower adds a picturesque feature to the natural beauty of Otsego Lake. Hardenburgh also designed the famous Plaza Hotel and the Dakota (the latter for Clark) in Manhattan. Today, Point Judith and Kingfisher Tower remain private property.

Top: Panoramic view of Otsego Lake, 1901–1902. The photographer used Kingfisher Tower as a point of interest in the foreground, just as envisioned by Edward Clark, who commissioned the tower. Three Mile Point is visible on the far side of the lake.

Bottom: Kingfisher Tower from the nearby shore, framed by a group of picturesque trees.

Opposite: Point Judith in early autumn, from the porch of the private camp built by Edward Clark in the 1870s.

Above: This duck's-eye view of Point Judith reveals aquatic plant life.

Opposite: The private mahogany launch *Narra Mattah,*
commissioned in 1902 by Elizabeth Severin Clark, at the tower's lakeside dock.

Above: Overhanging tree on the shoreline south of Point Judith.

Opposite: The shoreline in winter, a sculpture of snow, ice, and rock.

Following pages: The *Glimmerglass* in full autumn regalia, from Point Judith to Star Field.

Above: A lone sailboat on the shore.

Opposite: The camp at Point Judith, looking south to Cooperstown.

FAIRY SPRING

"...and yonder little fountain
that you see
gushing from the thicket,
and which comes
glancing like diamonds
into the lake,
is called the 'Fairy Spring.'"

Home as Found, Chapter XIV
James Fenimore Cooper

Otsego Lake from Fairy Spring, ca. 1880.

123

FAIRY SPRING

airy Spring, a short distance from Cooperstown on the east side of the lake, has provided literary inspiration and recreational opportunities for many years. Several caves near the spring have been associated with the exploits of Natty Bumppo, hero of Cooper's *Leatherstocking Tales*. Local tradition identifies a cleft about a mile north of the spring as the site of his fictional cave. Natty leads his companions through the cave to safety when a forest fire burns over Mount Vision.

> *...the experience of Natty conducted them to an opening through the rocks, where, with a little difficulty, they soon descended to another terrace, and emerged at once into a tolerably clear atmosphere.*
>
> The Pioneers,
> James Fenimore Cooper

Above the Spring lies Lakewood Cemetery, founded in 1856 during the American Rural Cemetery movement. The cemetery was designed to be a picturesque park as well as a burial site. With scenic vistas of the lake, Lakewood Cemetery became such an attraction that a steamboat landing was established to handle the large number of visitors. In 1860, a 25-foot tall memorial to James Fenimore Cooper was placed just inside the main entrance. The Leatherstocking Monument added another attraction to the natural beauty of Lakewood.

Fairy Spring Park opened in 1937 below the actual spring on land that was donated by Robert Sterling Clark. This popular park, run by the Village of Cooperstown, has partially terraced wooded grounds, gravel paths, picnicking facilities, and an open dock for swimming. It is still used by residents and visitors alike.

Above: Natty Bumppo's Cave, ca. 1910.

Right: Swimmers at Fairy Spring Park, ca. 1950.

Opposite: Fairy Spring Park is a shady, pine-covered hillside with an expansive view to the west.

Above: The westward orientation of the park offers fantastic sunsets.

Opposite: The shoreline near Fairy Spring, where trees and roots abruptly give way to the water.

Above and opposite: The dock at Fairy Spring before the arrival
of swimmers (above) and again after the end of the season (right).

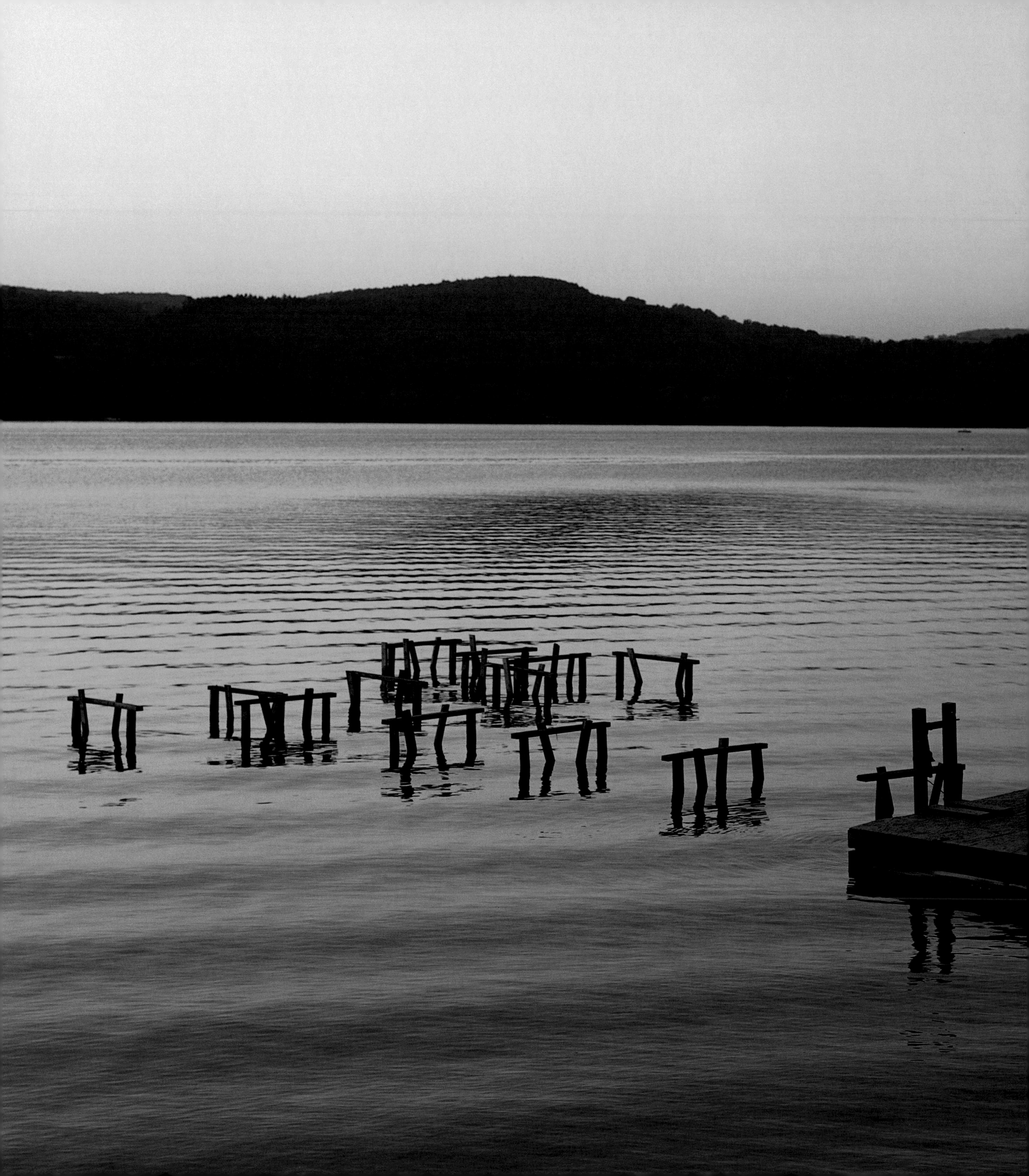

Above: Pine trees leaning precariously over the water's edge.

Opposite: A quiet dock at a camp south of Fairy Spring, near Cooperstown.

Above: The Caretaker's Cottage at Fairy Spring.

Opposite: The park in winter.

Above: On the hillside near Fairy Spring is an open field, near the
farm where Cooper did much of his writing. The clearing gets its name, Star Field,
from the distinctive shape it takes when viewed from the south.

Opposite: Lakewood Cemetery overlooks Otsego Lake from above Fairy Spring.
The Leatherstocking Monument, a tribute to James Fenimore Cooper from his fellow writers,
is one of the cemetery's most recognizable landmarks.

COUNCIL ROCK

*"The rock was not large,
being merely some
five or six feet high, only half
of which elevation rose
above the lake. The incessant
washing of the water
for centuries had so rounded
its summit, that it
resembled a large beehive
in shape, its form
being more than usually
regular and even."*

The Deerslayer, Chapter III

Photographer Arthur J. Telfer in the *Meta*
at the Clinton Dam marker, ca. 1910.

COUNCIL ROCK

Above: Council Rock in a ca. 1900 postcard.

Council Rock stands alone at the southern end of Otsego Lake. Deposited by glaciers, the rock lies at the head of the Susquehanna River, which flows more than 400 miles south before emptying in the Chesapeake Bay in Maryland.

Rising just a few feet above the water, the rock served as a landmark and meeting place for Native Americans. In *The Deerslayer*, Hurry Harry and Deerslayer use the rock to find the river's source, where their friends have hidden their boat, The Ark.

Called Otsego Rock earlier in the nineteenth century, the landmark was renamed "Council Rock" about 1870, when many areas around the lake were given names inspired by Cooper's *Leatherstocking Tales*.

In 1937, the Cooperstown Lake and Valley Garden Club built a flight of steps and a lake-level terrace to provide a view of Council Rock and the lake. Twenty years later, Paul F. Cooper, grandson of James Fenimore Cooper, gave a parcel of land at the foot of the steps to form Council Rock Park.

Across the river from Council Rock is a monument to the 1779 Sullivan-Clinton Campaign, the largest expedition to that date against the Indians of North America. That summer, General Clinton led an expedition of 1,500 Continental troops down Otsego Lake to join General Sullivan further south in an attack against Iroquois allied with British troops during the American Revolution. Clinton had a dam built across the entrance to the river to gradually raise the lake level. When the dam was broken the troops rode the surge of water downstream. To commemorate Clinton's Dam, the Otsego Chapter of the Daughters of the American Revolution erected the monument near the eastern shore of the river in 1901. A mortar tops the monument.

Bottom: Local residents portraying Leatherstocking, Chingachcook, and George Washington at the Cooperstown Centennial, 1907.

Opposite: Council Rock today, on a still morning.

Top: The lawn at Council Rock Park, looking across
the Susquehanna toward the Clinton Dam Monument.

Bottom: Unveiling of the Clinton Dam monument, 1901. The Daughters of the American Revolution
dedicated this monument to the Clinton-Sullivan Campaign of 1779.

Opposite: The edge of Council Rock Park in winter,
looking northward up the lake.

Above: Monument erected by the Daughters of the American Revolution
in 1901 to commemorate Clinton's Dam.

Opposite: The Susquehanna River originates at Council Rock Park, where the water
from Otsego Lake begins its 400-mile journey south to the Chesapeake Bay.

Above: Mallards stream through the mist past Council Rock.

Opposite: Canada geese make their way north from the mouth of the Susquehanna.

Above and opposite: The park in winter, like so many other areas around Otsego Lake, is a tranquil landscape of icicles and wide open spaces shrouded in snow.

ABOUT THE PHOTOGRAPHER

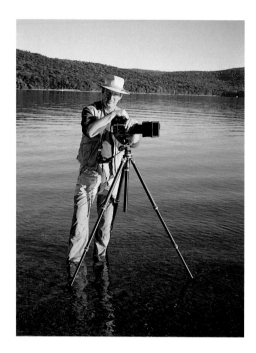

Richard S. Duncan
Photograph by Pamela Jane Welch

Bottom: Seagulls flock at the end
of a narrow peninsula on the grounds
of the former Mohican Manor.

Richard S. Duncan was born in Catskill, New York. He attended Manlius Military School, Rhode Island School of Design and was an apprentice to French painter Jacques Fabert. He also attended The School of the Museum of Fine Arts, Boston.

Richard's work has appeared in a number of books, here and abroad, and is in many private collections. He has had a number of shows around the country. In the summer of 2005, his photographs of Otsego Lake will be on exhibit at The Farmers' Museum.

The majority of the photographs are taken with a Hasselblad, a medium format camera that produces 2¼ x 2¼ inch transparencies. The lenses are 50mm, 120 macro and a 250mm for the medium format camera. Some images were made with a Contax T2 (a 35mm camera); others with a Leica digital camera used for 'sketching.' The film is Kodak Professional Ektachrome transparency film for the Hasselblad, and Kodachrome film for the 35mm camera. Polarizing filters are employed from time to time to strengthen colors.

ACKNOWLEDGEMENTS

Richard S. Duncan

This project would not have happened without the generosity of a number of people who allowed me to walk around their property in order for me to get the best angles for photographs. There were also many people who shared their stories of the lake that enlivened my viewpoint. A number of people took me out in their boats so I could get a different perspective of the lake. To all, I thank you; I could not have done it without your help.

I want to especially thank Jane Forbes Clark for her contributions to this project. Her generosity in allowing me to wander across her properties searching for interesting views, the meetings, the encouragements and her belief in the quality of my work, helped to inspire me.

Many thanks to Paul D'Ambrosio for enduring picture after picture, month after month. He met monthly with me, encouraging and guiding me through the whole project while trying to organize the piles of my slides. It was a pleasure to have his assistance. He helped make it happen.

It takes many people to do a project well. Thanks to Nadeau Design Associates – and especially Rich Nadeau for "polishing the nickel" and making me look good.

At home, my partner, Pamela Jane Welch was dealing with the many day-to-day problems while I "played the artist." This freed me up to be able to concentrate on taking pictures. Her love and support were instrumental to the success of this project. Pam would even wander with me out across the ice on freezing winter days, encouraging me with her presence. Thank You.

Without the guidance over the years of Kwan Sai-Hung in preparing my spirit and body I would not have been able to handle a golden opportunity such as this. His patience and unconditional training has helped add depth to my character, which in turn enriches the depth of my work.

Mallards feeding in shallow water near Cooperstown.

Below: Sunset over Otsego Lake.

ACKNOWLEDGEMENTS

Paul S. D'Ambrosio

A group of plastic beach toys, seen on a clear autumn day, are the only remnants of a busy summer at Three Mile Point.

In the summer of 2003 Richard Duncan approached The Farmers' Museum with an idea for a project that seemed long overdue; a complete contemporary photographic record of Otsego Lake. We have, in the collections of the New York State Historical Association, many historic photographs of the lake taken by Washington G. Smith, Arthur J. Telfer, and others, but it quickly became evident that there had been no systematic photographic record of Otsego Lake in at least fifty years. We approached Jane Forbes Clark, Chairman of the Museum's Board of Directors, and she immediately gave the project her enthusiastic support. To Richard and to Jane, therefore, The Farmers' Museum owes an immense debt of gratitude. This book simply would not have been possible without Richard's keen eye and Jane's encouragement, support, and guidance.

We are also grateful to Henry S. F. Cooper, Jr., a tireless advocate of the lake and a source of much inspiration to us. Henry's eloquent tribute to Otsego Lake, written for *Heritage* magazine on the occasion of the exhibition opening, is fittingly republished here as an introduction. We also thank Suzan D. Friedlander for her extensive research and early drafts which formed the basis of much of the book text.

We also extend our sincere thanks to the following individuals for their invaluable support of this exhibition: Matthew Albright, Scottie Baker; Andy Baugnet; Jeanie Bennett-O'Dea; Richard Davies; Noel Drese; Lea Foster; Martha H. Frey; Carl Good; Dr. Willard Harman; Tom Krieg; Hugh MacDougall; Michael and Cory Moffat; Nicholas Palevsky; Dr. Theodore Peters, Jr.; David Peterson; Jane Prior; Jessie Ravage; Suzanne Soden; Dr. Robert Titus; Eugene Tuite; Marybeth Vargha; and Michael Willis.

Likewise, we are grateful to the following organizations for their support of this project: Advocates for Springfield; Biological Field Station, SUNY Oneonta; Cooperstown Water Board; Friends of Hyde Hall; General Clinton Canoe Regatta Museum; Glimmerglass Opera; Glimmerglass State Park; Hyde Bay Association; Nadeau Design Associates; National Resources Conservation Service; Otsego County GIS; Otsego County Planning Department; Otsego County Soil and Water Conservation District; Otsego Lake Association; Otsego Lake Water Quality Committee; Otsego Lake Watershed Supervisory Committee; Otsego Land Trust; Otsego 2000, Inc.; Paul F. Cooper, Jr. Archives, Hartwick College; Seifert Signs, Inc.; Springfield Historical Society; Village of Cooperstown; Yager Museum, Hartwick College; and Zaveral Racing Equipment, Inc.